cupcakes, cookies
& coffee cakes

Easy dishes to cook at home

First published in 2009
Love Food ® is an imprint of Parragon Books Ltd

Parragon
Queen Street House
4 Queen Street
Bath BA1 1HE, UK

Copyright © Parragon Books Ltd 2009

Love Food ® and the accompanying heart device is a trademark of Parragon Books Ltd

ISBN: 978-1-4075-8102-6

Printed in Malaysia

Designed by Talking Design
Cover text and introduction by Lorraine Turner

Notes for the reader
This book uses imperial, metric, and US cup measurements. Follow the same units of measurement throughout; do not mix imperial and metric. All spoon measurements are level: teaspoons are assumed to be 5 ml, and tablespoons are assumed to be 15 ml. Unless otherwise stated, milk is assumed to be whole, eggs and individual vegetables, such as potatoes, are medium, and pepper is freshly ground black pepper.

The times given are an approximate guide only. Preparation times differ according to the techniques used by different people and the cooking times may also vary from those given as a result of the type of oven used. Optional ingredients, variations, or serving suggestions have not been included in the calculations.

Recipes using raw or very lightly cooked eggs should be avoided by infants, the elderly, pregnant women, convalescents, and anyone with a chronic condition. Pregnant and breastfeeding women are advised to avoid eating peanuts and peanut products. People with nut allergies should be aware that some of the prepared ingredients used in the recipes in this book may contain nuts. Always check the packaging before use.

Contents

introduction

Coffee has experienced a revival these days, and the multitude of coffee shops springing up in every town is a testimony to its increasing popularity. Along with this renewed thirst has come the rebirth of its much-loved partner—cake. What could be better than nibbling on a mouthwatering piece of sticky chocolate brownie while sipping a cup of delicious cappuccino?

For informal entertaining, nothing can beat the taste and smell of a fresh brew and lovingly prepared sweet treats. Coffee and cakes are also the perfect way to round off a dinner party. When you're not entertaining, why not snatch a few moments to yourself, put your feet up, and treat yourself to a cup of hot steaming mocha and some irresistible sponge layer cake?

Coffee, and various teas, have a strong flavor, so the cakes or accompanying desserts that you choose must have a sufficiently strong flavor of their own in order not to be overwhelmed. Chocolate is the perfect partner for coffee: it creates a rich, dark taste explosion that will tantalize your taste buds and those of your guests. Cakes containing different kinds of nuts, such as walnuts, pecans, and almonds, are also ideal. The flavor of coconut goes well with coffee, and don't forget that most luxurious partner of all—cream—a combination made in heaven!

Preparing and cooking cakes

Making wonderful cakes, cupcakes, cookies, and bars is easy. If you have children, they will enjoy helping you to bake them too, making even lighter work! Simply give them an apron and a wooden spoon and they can help you mix the ingredients. They will also have fun decorating the cakes with sprinkles, candied cherries, chocolate chips, colored icing, marshmallows, coffee beans, candies, and whatever else appeals to the imagination. Just remember to allow a little more time for cleaning up afterward!

Here are a few simple tips to help you create successful cakes every time:

- Do not store your flour for too long, especially self-rising flour, or you could end up with a sunken cake.

- About 30 minutes before you start, bring all of the ingredients to room temperature to make beating and whipping easier.

- Preheat the oven while you are preparing the batter, so that the oven is sufficiently hot before you put in the cake batter. This will help your cake to rise quickly and easily.

- Sift your flour twice to incorporate more air and thus create a lighter cake.

- Follow the recipe instructions exactly. For example, some instructions are designed to enable more air to get into the mixture and ensure a lighter cake.

- Avoid opening the oven door until the last few minutes of the cooking time or your cake will sink.

- When using chocolate, opt for bars that contain at least 70% cocoa solids.

- Remember that oven temperatures and cooking times vary, so you may need to make more than one batch of cakes to get used to how your oven functions. Make any necessary adjustments, note any changes on your favorite recipes, and keep for future reference.

Essential equipment

You don't need lots of special equipment to prepare and bake exciting cakes—just a few basic items will get you started.

At least one large mixing bowl is essential. You will also need a selection of cake pans. A springform pan is ideal for large cakes, and you will find a couple of 12-cup muffin pans very helpful for making smaller cakes. You will also need a couple of layer cake pans for baking two-tier sponge cakes. You can add other pans, such as a jelly roll pan, as your time and budget allow.

Other items you will need include a set of measuring cups and spoons, a sifter, a whisk, a grater, a wooden spoon, and a spatula. An electric hand mixer or food processor will save you a lot of time when preparing the cake batter, but is not essential.

classic
cakes

Sponge
Layer Cake

SERVES 8

¾ cup unsalted butter, softened,
  plus extra for greasing
scant 1 cup superfine sugar
3 eggs, beaten
scant 1¼ cups self-rising flour
pinch of salt
3 tbsp raspberry jelly
1 tbsp superfine or confectioners'
  sugar

Preheat the oven to 350°F/180°C. Grease 2 x 8-inch/20-cm round
shallow cake pans and line the bottoms with parchment paper.

Cream together the butter and sugar in a bowl until pale and fluffy.
Add the beaten eggs, a little at a time, beating well after each addition.

Sift the flour and salt together, then gently fold into the batter using
a metal spoon or a spatula. Divide the batter between the prepared
pans and smooth the surfaces.

Bake both cakes on the same shelf in the center of the preheated oven
for 25–30 minutes, until well risen, golden brown, and beginning to
shrink from the sides of each pan.

Let stand in the pans for 1 minute. Using a palette knife, loosen the
cakes from around the edge of each pan. Turn out the cakes onto a
clean dish towel, remove the lining paper, and invert onto a cooling
rack (this prevents the cooling rack from marking the top of the cakes).

When completely cool, sandwich together with the jelly and sprinkle
with the sugar. The cake is delicious when freshly baked, but any
remaining cake can be stored in an airtight tin for up to 1 week.

Chocolate
Fudge Cake

SERVES 8

3/4 cup unsalted butter, softened,
   plus extra for greasing
generous 1 cup superfine sugar
3 eggs, beaten
3 tbsp dark corn syrup
3 tbsp ground almonds
generous 1 cup self-rising flour
pinch of salt
1/4 cup unsweetened cocoa

Frosting

8 oz/225 g semisweet chocolate,
   broken into pieces
1/4 cup dark brown sugar
1 cup unsalted butter, diced
5 tbsp evaporated milk
1/2 tsp vanilla extract

Grease 2 x 8-inch/20-cm round cake pans and line the bottoms with parchment paper. To make the frosting, place the chocolate, brown sugar, butter, evaporated milk, and vanilla extract in a heavy-bottom pan. Heat gently, stirring constantly, until melted. Pour into a bowl and let cool. Cover and let chill in the refrigerator for 1 hour, or until spreadable.

Preheat the oven to 350°F/180°C. Place the butter and superfine sugar in a bowl and beat together until light and fluffy. Gradually beat in the eggs. Stir in the corn syrup and ground almonds. Sift the flour, salt, and cocoa into a separate bowl, then fold into the cake batter. Add a little water, if necessary, to make a dropping consistency. Spoon the cake batter into the prepared pans and bake in the preheated oven for 30–35 minutes, or until springy to the touch and a skewer inserted in the center comes out clean.

Let stand in the pans for 5 minutes, then turn out onto wire racks to cool completely. When the cakes are cold, sandwich them together with half the frosting. Spread the remaining frosting over the top and sides of the cake, swirling it to give a frosted appearance.

Carrot
Cake

SERVES 8

butter, for greasing

scant 1 cup light brown sugar

3 eggs

¾ cup sunflower or corn oil

1 cup coarsely grated carrots

2 ripe bananas, mashed

⅓ cup chopped walnuts

2 cups all-purpose flour

½ tsp salt

1 tsp baking soda

2 tsp baking powder

Frosting

scant 1 cup cream cheese

½ tsp vanilla extract

generous 1 cup confectioners' sugar

2 tbsp chopped walnuts

Preheat the oven to 350°F/180°C. Grease a 9-inch/23-cm round springform cake pan and line the bottom with parchment paper. Place the brown sugar, eggs, oil, carrots, bananas, and walnuts in a bowl. Sift in the flour, salt, baking soda, and baking powder. Beat the batter until smooth.

Turn the batter into the prepared pan and bake in the preheated oven for 1 hour 5 minutes, or until well risen and golden brown and a skewer inserted into the center comes out clean. Let cool in the pan for 10 minutes, then turn out and peel off the lining paper. Transfer to a wire rack to cool completely.

To make the frosting, place the cream cheese and vanilla extract in a bowl and beat well to soften. Beat in the confectioners' sugar a tablespoon at a time, until smooth. Swirl over the cake and sprinkle the chopped walnuts on top. Let stand in a cool place for the frosting to harden slightly before serving.

Apple
Cake

SERVES 8

3 apples, peeled, cored, and sliced

1 cup unsalted butter, diced, plus
  extra for greasing

½ cup superfine sugar

½ cup packed raw brown sugar

½ tsp vanilla extract

½ tsp ground cinnamon

4 eggs

scant ¾ cup light brown self-rising
  flour

scant 1 cup white self-rising flour

1 tsp baking powder

1 tbsp honey

3–4 slices dried apple, chopped

Preheat the oven to 350°F/180°C. Grease a 9-inch/23-cm round cake pan and line with parchment paper. Arrange the apple slices in the bottom of the prepared pan.

Put all the remaining ingredients, except the honey and dried apple, in a food processor and pulse until well combined. Pour the cake batter over the apples and bake in the preheated oven for 1 hour, or until golden brown and a skewer inserted into the center of the cake comes out clean.

Remove from the oven and let cool in the pan, then invert onto a plate and remove the lining paper. Turn back over onto a serving plate. Spread the top of the cake with the honey and sprinkle over the dried apple.

Clementine
Cake

SERVES 8

pared rind of 2 clementines

¾ cup butter, softened, plus extra
   for greasing

scant 1 cup superfine sugar

3 eggs, lightly beaten

scant 1¼ cups self-rising flour

3 tbsp ground almonds

3 tbsp light cream

Glaze & Topping

6 tbsp clementine juice

2 tbsp superfine sugar

3 white sugar lumps, crushed

Preheat the oven to 350°F/180°C. Grease a 7-inch/18-cm round cake pan and line the bottom with parchment paper.

Finely chop the clementine rind. Cream together the butter, sugar, and clementine rind in a bowl until pale and fluffy.

Add the beaten eggs, a little at a time, beating well after each addition. Gently fold in the flour, ground almonds, and cream. Spoon the batter into the prepared pan.

Bake in the preheated oven for 55–60 minutes, or until a skewer inserted into the center comes out clean. Let cool slightly.

Meanwhile, to make the glaze, put the clementine juice in a small pan with the superfine sugar over low–medium heat. Bring to a boil, then reduce the heat and simmer for 5 minutes.

Turn out the cake onto a cooling rack. Drizzle the glaze over the cake until it has been absorbed and sprinkle with the crushed sugar lumps. Let cool completely before serving.

Lemon
Drizzle Cake

SERVES 8

butter, for greasing

1³/₄ cups all-purpose flour

2 tsp baking powder

1 cup superfine sugar

4 eggs

²/₃ cup sour cream

grated rind of 1 large lemon

4 tbsp lemon juice

²/₃ cup sunflower oil

Syrup

4 tbsp confectioners' sugar

3 tbsp lemon juice

Preheat the oven to 350°F/180°C. Lightly grease an 8-inch/20-cm loose-bottom round cake pan and line the bottom with parchment paper.

Sift the flour and baking powder into a mixing bowl and stir in the superfine sugar. In a separate bowl, whisk the eggs, sour cream, lemon rind, lemon juice, and oil together.

Pour the egg mixture into the dry ingredients and mix well until evenly combined.

Pour the batter into the prepared pan and bake in the preheated oven for 45–60 minutes, or until risen and golden brown.

Meanwhile, to make the syrup, mix together the confectioners' sugar and lemon juice in a small pan. Stir over low heat until just beginning to bubble and turn syrupy.

As soon as the cake comes out of the oven, prick the surface with a fine skewer, then brush the syrup over the top. Let the cake cool completely in the pan before turning out and serving.

Almond & Hazelnut
Gâteau

SERVES 8

butter, for greasing

4 eggs

½ cup superfine sugar

½ cup ground almonds

½ cup ground hazelnuts

5½ tbsp all-purpose flour

scant ½ cup slivered almonds

confectioners' sugar, for dusting

Filling

3½ oz/100 g semisweet chocolate,
  broken into pieces

1 tbsp unsalted butter

1¼ cups heavy cream

Preheat the oven to 375°F/190°C. Grease 2 x 7-inch/18-cm round shallow cake pans and line the bottoms with parchment paper. Whisk the eggs and superfine sugar together for 10 minutes, or until light and foamy and the beater leaves a trail that lasts a few seconds when lifted. Fold in the ground almonds and hazelnuts, sift the flour, and fold in with a metal spoon or spatula.

Pour into the prepared pans. Sprinkle the slivered almonds over the top of one of the cakes, then bake both cakes in the preheated oven for 15–20 minutes, or until springy to the touch. Let cool in the pans for 5 minutes, then turn out onto wire racks to cool completely.

To make the filling, melt the chocolate in a heatproof bowl set over a pan of gently simmering water and stir in the butter. Let cool. Whip the cream until holding its shape, then fold in the chocolate mixture until mixed.

Place the cake without the extra almonds on a serving plate and spread the filling over it. Let set slightly, then place the almond-topped cake on top of the filling and let chill in the refrigerator for 1 hour. Dust with confectioners' sugar before serving.

a little
something

Drizzled
Honey Cupcakes

MAKES 12

scant ⅔ cup self-rising flour

¼ tsp ground cinnamon

pinch of ground cloves

pinch of grated nutmeg

6 tbsp unsalted butter, softened

generous ½ cup superfine sugar

1 tbsp honey

finely grated rind of 1 orange

2 eggs, lightly beaten

¾ cup walnut pieces, finely chopped

Topping

2 tbsp finely chopped walnuts

¼ tsp ground cinnamon

2 tbsp honey

juice of 1 orange

Preheat the oven to 375°F/190°C. Put 12 paper liners in a muffin pan, or put 12 double-layer paper liners on a baking sheet.

Sift together the flour, cinnamon, cloves, and nutmeg into a bowl. Put the butter and sugar in a separate bowl and beat together until light and fluffy. Beat in the honey and orange rind, then gradually add the beaten eggs, beating well after each addition. Using a metal spoon, fold in the flour mixture. Stir in the walnuts, then spoon the batter into the paper liners.

Bake the cupcakes in the preheated oven for 20 minutes, or until well risen and golden brown. Transfer to a wire rack and let cool.

To make the topping, mix together the walnuts and cinnamon. Put the honey and orange juice in a pan and heat gently, stirring, until combined.

When the cupcakes have almost cooled, prick the tops all over with a fork or skewer and drizzle with the warm honey mixture. Sprinkle the walnut mixture over the top of each cupcake and serve warm or cold.

Mochaccino Brownies
with White Mocha Sauce

MAKES 9

½ cup unsalted butter, plus extra for
   greasing
4 oz/115 g semisweet chocolate,
   broken into pieces
2 tbsp strong black coffee
1¼ cups superfine sugar
3 eggs, beaten
¾ cup all-purpose flour
⅓ cup milk chocolate chips
½ cup toasted walnuts,
   skinned and chopped
chopped walnuts, to decorate

Sauce

scant ½ cup heavy cream
3 oz/85 g white chocolate,
   broken into pieces
1 tbsp strong black coffee

Preheat the oven to 350°F/180°C. Grease a 9-inch/23-cm square cake pan and line with baking parchment.

Place the butter, semisweet chocolate, and coffee in a pan over low heat and stir until just melted and combined. Let cool slightly.

Whisk in the sugar and eggs. Beat in the flour, chocolate chips, and walnuts. Pour into the prepared pan.

Bake in the preheated oven for 30–35 minutes, until just firm but still moist inside. Let cool in the pan, then cut into squares.

Meanwhile, make the sauce by placing all the ingredients in a small pan over low heat, stirring occasionally, until melted and smooth.

Place the brownies on individual plates and spoon the warm sauce over the top. Decorate with chopped walnuts.

Chocolate Chip
Oaties

MAKES 20

½ cup unsalted butter, softened,
   plus extra for greasing

½ cup light brown sugar

1 egg

1 cup rolled oats

1 tbsp milk

1 tsp vanilla extract

scant 1 cup all-purpose flour

1 tbsp unsweetened cocoa

½ tsp baking powder

6 oz/175 g semisweet chocolate,
   chopped

6 oz/175 g milk chocolate, chopped

Preheat the oven to 350°F/180°C. Grease 2 large baking sheets. Place the butter and sugar in a bowl and beat together with a wooden spoon until light and fluffy.

Beat in the egg, then add the oats, milk, and vanilla extract. Beat together until well blended. Sift the flour, cocoa, and baking powder into the mixture and stir. Stir in the chocolate.

Place tablespoonfuls of the cookie dough on the prepared baking sheets and flatten slightly with a fork. Bake in the preheated oven for 15 minutes, or until slightly risen and firm. Remove from the oven and let cool on the baking sheets for 2 minutes, then transfer to wire racks to cool completely.

Hazelnut
Chocolate Crunch

MAKES 12

generous 2 cups rolled oats

⅓ cup hazelnuts, lightly toasted and
  chopped

generous ⅓ cup all-purpose flour

½ cup unsalted butter,
  plus extra for greasing

scant ½ cup light brown sugar

2 tbsp dark corn syrup

⅓ cup semisweet chocolate chips

Preheat the oven to 350°F/180°C. Grease a 9-inch/23-cm square baking pan. Mix together the oats, hazelnuts, and flour in a large bowl.

Place the butter, sugar, and corn syrup in a large pan and heat gently until the sugar has dissolved. Pour in the dry ingredients and mix well. Stir in the chocolate chips.

Turn into the prepared pan and bake in the preheated oven for 20–25 minutes, or until golden brown and firm to the touch. Using a knife, mark into bars or triangles and let cool in the pan. When cool, cut with a sharp knife before carefully removing them from the pan.

Mixed Fruit
Rolls

MAKES 9

1½ cups white bread flour,
  plus extra for dusting

½ tsp salt

1½ tsp active dry yeast

1 tsp superfine sugar

2 tbsp butter, diced, plus extra
  for greasing

½ cup lukewarm milk

1 egg, beaten

oil, for oiling

¾ cup confectioners' sugar

Filling

generous ½ cup light brown sugar

⅔ cup luxury mixed dried fruit

1 tsp ground allspice

4 tbsp butter, softened

Grease a 7-inch/18-cm square cake pan. Sift the flour and salt together into a warmed bowl, then stir in the yeast and superfine sugar. Rub in the butter with your fingertips until the mixture resembles breadcrumbs. Make a well in the center. Mix the milk and egg together and add to the well. Mix to form a soft dough. Turn out the dough onto a lightly floured counter and knead for 5–10 minutes, or until smooth and elastic. Put in an oiled bowl, cover with plastic wrap, and let rise in a warm place for 1 hour, or until doubled in size. Turn out the dough again and knead lightly for 1 minute. Roll out into a rectangle measuring 12 x 9 inches/30 x 23 cm.

To make the filling, mix together the brown sugar, dried fruit, and allspice in a bowl. Spread the dough with the butter and sprinkle the fruit mixture on top. Roll up, starting from one long edge. Cut into 9 slices and arrange, cut-side up, in the prepared pan. Cover with oiled plastic wrap and let prove in a warm place for 45 minutes. Preheat the oven to 375°F/190°C.

Bake in the preheated oven for 30 minutes, or until golden. Let cool in the pan for 10 minutes, then transfer, in one piece, to a wire rack and let cool completely. Sift the confectioners' sugar into a bowl and stir in enough water to make a thin glaze. Brush over the rolls and let set. Pull the rolls apart to serve.

Blueberry Bran
Muffins

MAKES 10

generous 1 cup white
  all-purpose flour

scant ¾ cup light brown
  self-rising flour

1 tbsp oat bran

2 tsp baking powder

½ tsp baking soda

pinch of salt

¼ cup packed raw brown sugar

1 tbsp honey

1 large egg

scant 1 cup buttermilk

generous 1 cup fresh blueberries

Preheat the oven to 350°F/180°C. Place 10 paper liners in a muffin pan. Mix together the flours, bran, baking powder, baking soda, and salt in a bowl and stir in the sugar. Whisk the honey, egg, and buttermilk together in a pitcher.

Pour the wet ingredients into the dry ingredients and stir briefly to combine. Don't overmix—the batter should still be a little lumpy. Fold in the blueberries.

Spoon the batter into the paper liners and bake in the preheated oven for 20 minutes, or until risen and lightly browned.

Remove the muffins from the oven and let cool in the pan. Serve warm or cold.

pure

indulgence

Chocolate & Cherry
Gâteau

SERVES 8

2 lb/900 g fresh cherries, pitted and halved

1¼ cups superfine sugar

scant ½ cup cherry brandy

¾ cup all-purpose flour

5 tbsp unsweetened cocoa

½ tsp baking powder

4 eggs

3 tbsp unsalted butter, melted, plus extra for greasing

4 cups heavy cream

grated semisweet chocolate and whole fresh cherries, to decorate

Preheat the oven to 350°F/180°C. Grease and line a 9-inch/23-cm round springform cake pan. Place the cherries in a saucepan, add 3 tablespoons of the sugar and the cherry brandy, and bring to a simmer over medium heat. Simmer for 5 minutes. Drain, reserving the syrup. In a large bowl, sift together the flour, cocoa, and baking powder.

Place the eggs in a heatproof bowl and beat in ¾ cup of the remaining sugar. Place the bowl over a saucepan of simmering water and beat for 6 minutes, or until thickened. Remove from the heat, then gradually fold in the flour mixture and the melted butter. Spoon into the prepared cake pan and bake in the preheated oven for 40 minutes. Remove from the oven and let cool in the pan.

Turn out the cake and cut in half horizontally. Mix the heavy cream and the remaining sugar together and whip lightly until soft peaks form. Spread the reserved syrup over the cut sides of the cake, then top with half the whipped cream. Arrange the cherries over half of the cake, then place the other half on top. Cover the top of the cake with the remaining whipped cream, sprinkle over the grated chocolate, and decorate with the whole fresh cherries.

Raspberry
Vacherin

SERVES 10

3 egg whites

¾ cup superfine sugar

1 tsp cornstarch

1 oz/25 g semisweet chocolate,
   grated

Filling

6 oz/175 g semisweet chocolate,
   broken into pieces

2 cups heavy cream, whipped

2 cups fresh raspberries

Preheat the oven to 275°F/140°C. Draw
3 rectangles, each measuring 4 x 10 inches/
10 x 25 cm, on sheets of parchment paper, and
place on baking sheets.

Whip the egg whites until soft peaks form, then
gradually whisk in half of the sugar and continue whipping until the
mixture is very stiff and glossy. Carefully fold in the remaining sugar,
the cornstarch, and grated chocolate with a metal spoon.

Spoon the meringue mixture into a pastry bag fitted with a
½-inch/1-cm plain tip and pipe lines across the rectangles. Bake in
the preheated oven for 1½ hours, changing the position of the baking
sheets halfway through. Turn off the oven and let the meringues cool
completely. Peel away the parchment paper.

Place the chocolate in a heatproof bowl set over a pan of gently
simmering water and stir until melted. Spread most of the melted
chocolate over 2 of the meringue layers, reserving a little for
decoration. Let set. Place 1 chocolate-coated meringue on a plate and
top with about one-third of the cream and raspberries. Gently place
the second chocolate-coated meringue on top and spread with half of
the remaining cream and raspberries. Place the last meringue on the
top and decorate with the remaining cream and raspberries. Drizzle
the remaining melted chocolate over the top and serve.

Brownie Bottom
Cheesecake

SERVES 10

Brownie Bottom

½ cup unsalted butter, plus extra for
  greasing

4 oz/115 g bittersweet chocolate,
  broken into pieces

1 cup superfine sugar

2 eggs, beaten

¼ cup milk

1 cup all-purpose flour

Topping

2¼ cups cream cheese

⅔ cup superfine sugar

3 eggs, beaten

1 tsp vanilla extract

½ cup plain yogurt

melted chocolate, for drizzling

strawberries dipped in melted
  chocolate, to serve

Preheat the oven to 350°F/180°C. Lightly grease a 9-inch/23-cm round springform cake pan.

Melt the butter and chocolate in a pan over low heat, stirring frequently, until smooth. Remove from the heat and beat in the sugar.

Add the eggs and milk, beating well. Stir in the flour, mixing just until blended. Spoon into the prepared pan, spreading evenly.

Bake in the preheated oven for 25 minutes. Remove from the oven while preparing the topping. Reduce the oven temperature to 325°F/160°C.

For the topping, beat together the cream cheese, sugar, eggs, and vanilla extract until well blended. Stir in the yogurt, then pour over the brownie bottom. Bake for an additional 45–55 minutes, or until the center is almost set.

Run a knife around the edge of the cake to loosen from the pan. Let cool before removing from the pan. Chill in the refrigerator for 4 hours or overnight before cutting into slices. Drizzle with melted chocolate and serve with chocolate-dipped strawberries.

Chocolate Berry
Dacquoise

SERVES 8

4 egg whites

1 cup superfine sugar

generous ½ cup ground hazelnuts

8 oz/225 g semisweet chocolate,
   broken into pieces

1½ cups heavy cream

2 tbsp Kirsch

2 cups mixed berries, such as
   strawberries, raspberries, and
   blueberries

Preheat the oven to 275°/140°C. Line 3 baking sheets with parchment paper and mark a 7-inch/18-cm circle on each. Whip the egg whites until very stiff, then gradually add the sugar, beating well after each addition. When all the sugar has been added, stir in the ground hazelnuts. Mix lightly until thoroughly incorporated.

Divide the meringue among the 3 baking sheets, then spread evenly within the circles. Bake in the preheated oven for 1 hour–1 hour 30 minutes, or until the meringues feel firm to the touch. Let cool.

Place the chocolate in a heavy-bottom pan with 1 cup of the cream and the Kirsch. Heat gently, stirring until melted and smooth. Remove from the heat and pour into a bowl. Let cool slightly, then chill for at least 2 hours, or until set. Once set, whip until light and fluffy.

Spread two-thirds of the chocolate mixture over 2 of the meringues and spread to the edges. Arrange most of the berries over the chocolate filling, reserving the remainder for decoration. Place the meringues one on top of the other, ending with the plain meringue.

Whip the remaining cream until stiff. Reserve a little for decoration, then use the remainder to spread around the sides. Spread the remaining chocolate mixture over the top. Pipe rosettes of the reserved cream around the top edge of the dacquoise. Chill for 2 hours before serving, decorated with the remaining berries.

Mississippi
Mud Pie

SERVES 8

Pie Dough

1½ cups all-purpose flour, plus extra
  for dusting

2 tbsp unsweetened cocoa

½ cup unsalted butter

2 tbsp superfine sugar

Filling

¾ cup unsalted butter

scant 1¾ cups dark brown sugar

4 eggs, lightly beaten

4 tbsp unsweetened cocoa, sifted

5½ oz/150 g semisweet chocolate,
  broken into pieces

1¼ cups light cream

1 tsp chocolate extract

Topping

scant 2 cups heavy cream, whipped

chocolate curls

To make the pie dough, sift the flour and cocoa into a bowl. Rub in the butter with your fingertips until the mixture resembles fine breadcrumbs. Stir in the superfine sugar and enough cold water to mix to a soft dough. Wrap the dough in plastic wrap and let chill in the refrigerator for 15 minutes.

Preheat the oven to 375°F/190°C. Roll out the dough on a lightly floured counter and use to line a 9-inch/23-cm round loose-bottom tart pan. Line with parchment paper and fill with dried beans. Bake in the preheated oven for 15 minutes. Remove from the oven and take out the paper and beans. Bake the pastry shell for an additional 10 minutes.

To make the filling, beat the butter and brown sugar together in a bowl and gradually beat in the eggs with the cocoa. Melt the chocolate and beat it into the mixture with the light cream and chocolate extract.

Reduce the oven temperature to 325°F/160°C. Pour the mixture into the pastry shell and bake for 45 minutes, or until the filling has set gently. Let cool completely, then transfer to a serving plate. Cover with the whipped cream and decorate with chocolate curls, then let chill until ready to serve.

Truffled Honey
Tart

SERVES 8

Pie Dough

generous ¾ cup all-purpose flour,
plus extra for dusting

pinch of salt

5 tbsp unsalted butter, chilled,
cut into pieces, plus extra
for greasing

1 tsp confectioners' sugar

Filling

1⅛ cups curd cheese

scant ½ cup cream cheese

½ cup heavy cream

1 egg

2 egg yolks

2 tbsp superfine sugar

4 tbsp flower honey, plus extra
for drizzling

sugared rose petals, to decorate

Grease a 9-inch/23-cm round loose-bottom tart pan. Sift the flour and salt into a food processor, add the butter, and process until the mixture resembles fine breadcrumbs. Tip into a bowl, then add the confectioners' sugar and enough cold water to mix to a soft dough.

Turn out onto a lightly floured counter and roll out the dough 3¼ inches/8 cm larger than the prepared pan. Carefully lift the dough into the pan and press to fit. Roll the rolling pin over the pan to neaten the edges and trim the excess dough. Line with parchment paper, fill with dried beans, and let chill in the refrigerator for 30 minutes. Meanwhile, preheat the oven to 375°F/190°C.

Remove the pastry shell from the refrigerator and bake in the preheated oven for 10 minutes, then remove the beans and paper and bake for an additional 5 minutes.

Mix the curd cheese, cream cheese, and cream together until smooth, then stir in the egg, egg yolks, sugar, and honey until completely smooth. Pour into the pastry shell and bake for 30 minutes. Remove from the oven and let cool in the pan for 10 minutes. Drizzle with a little honey and decorate with rose petals.